YOU'RE WORTH IT!

# YOU'RE WORTH IT!

TRE' BOHANNON

NEW DEGREE PRESS
COPYRIGHT © 2021 TRE' BOHANNON
*All rights reserved.*

YOU'RE WORTH IT!

ISBN   978-1-63730-995-7   *Paperback*
       978-1-63730-907-0   *Kindle Ebook*
       978-1-63730-945-2   *Ebook*

*I'm dedicating this book to my parents, Bo and Regenia. I am extremely grateful and appreciative of everything y'all have done for me. 381. I love you!*

# TABLE OF CONTENTS

———

# INTRODUCTION

———

December 17 of my second year of college started off like any other day. I had survived finals and was back at home for the first time in months. I woke up to the bright light of the Texas sun peeking through my curtains. As I slowly opened my eyes, I let out a yawn and stretched out my entire body. I slid myself out of the bed and made my way to the bathroom, but I didn't feel like I was ready to face the day. I hopped back under my warm covers and started watching videos on my phone.

After a few minutes, my mom knocked on my door and popped her head in.

"Tre'?" she asked gently.

I looked up from my phone. She had a worried expression on her face. Before I could ask what was wrong, she began again.

"Tre', are you happy?"

"What do you mean, Mom?"

"Well... it's kinda like you're just going through the motions. Ever since you went off to school, you don't act like yourself anymore."

The weight of her words fell heavy on my shoulders. She was right.

"No," I answered. "I'm not happy."

"Why not?" she asked, her voice shaking as tears began to well up in her eyes.

I could tell she was hurting, but there was nothing I could do to help her. I sighed and sat up in bed, terrified of letting her down by telling her the truth; I didn't really have an answer for her.

"I'm just not happy right now," I said. "But I will be happy... just not right now."

She left the room and shut the door. In that moment, I began to realize I was not living the life I wanted.

I no longer cared about school. I didn't want to leave the house, let alone my room. I felt unfulfilled and lost and wondered what it was I was doing in the world, just like everyone else trying to figure this life thing out, balance it all, be happy, and enjoy life.

I had never taken the time to consider or even think about my mental health. They were two words I had rarely ever heard paired together—never spoken aloud in my family, with my friends, or even at school. I didn't know this is where my energy should've been going. In all honesty, I didn't even know I was depressed or what depression was. All I knew was I was in that group of "one in ten young people who experience a period of major depression annually" (Magellan Health Insights).

Over the course of the next few years, I discovered how to combat depression and convert those negative thoughts and feelings of hopelessness into a positive mindset fueled by growth and self-love. It wasn't until a warm August day in Texas that I decided to write a book that would allow me to share my journey and, more importantly, bring value to others.

With the temperature on the brink of kissing 100 degrees, I decided to wait till that evening around sunset to go on my walk around the neighborhood. It had only been three months since I had graduated from Georgetown University. Since being home, one of the habits I began to do more frequently was walking outside. I saw it as a great way to stay active, clear my mind, and get out to take in the world and scenery. Each walk brought me peace, self-reflection, and the opportunity to learn myself and who I am.

Thank God the wind remembered who I was and embraced me as I took my first few steps out the front door. On this particular day, I was walking and listening—more specifically, listening to the birds singing their tunes around me while also listening to myself. I was thinking about where I was in my life, what I had already done, and what I was looking to accomplish.

*What's next for me?* I thought as I meticulously scrolled through each of my brain cells searching for the answer.

*Aha! I know it's always been a personal goal of mine to write my own book, but what would it even be about? Where do I begin? What do I even have to share with the world? I don't want to just write about anything, but rather something that I already focus on and that will benefit other people. I want to make it my own.*

Back to my thoughts I go. By this time, I had finished my second lap around the neighborhood with just enough sunlight to take one more trip.

The one common theme I had been thinking heavily about was my own development and mental health and how I could work on growing and making myself better every day.

I knew I was big on personal development—teaching myself, self-education, learning every day, wanting better and more out of life, and just having the insatiable desire to evolve as an individual inside and out.

This was it! This was my book!

The first thing I did with this decision was act on it. I hopped on LinkedIn and pinged Eric Koester. Eric is a Georgetown professor who I had met my freshman year at an entrepreneurship workshop. I listened to him speak about entrepreneurship, break down common myths, and explain what it is to be an entrepreneur. One of the things that really caught my attention was the class he taught at Georgetown. It was a book-writing course where students could write and publish their own book. I wasn't able to take his class during my time at school, but it was always in the back of my head. Fast forward to me finishing my walk. I immediately walked in the house and pinged him.

The message read, "Hi, Professor Koester! I hope you are doing well. My name is Tre' Bohannon, and I am a recent grad from Georgetown (MSB). Unfortunately, I never got to take your class, but I just wanted to take the time to connect and formally introduce myself. Do you have time for a quick call sometime this week?"

I didn't really know when I'd write my book, but I knew that I would write one and turn my dream into a reality. Surprisingly, it was a lot sooner than I had even imagined. Eric replied back telling me about an "open-source" program where I could write my book. And when God tosses you that alley-oop, you better finish it! I looked at the details of the program, filled out the form, and was on a call with Eric within a week.

I began my research, started speaking with more young adults, and reached out to the mental health professionals and counselors I would be honored to interview and build relationships with. Everything was clicking, all cylinders were connecting, and I knew it was meant to be.

Throughout this book, I will be sharing some of my personal stories, lessons I've learned and continue to use in my everyday life, as well as actionable exercises and tips you can immediately apply in your own life. I wanted to take the time to be more vulnerable and open about stories and situations I'm usually uncomfortable sharing with others in order to provide you the keys, gems, and resources that have helped me live a happier life. My goals for this book are to encourage growth and personal development, help promote a more positive mindset, and shed light on the importance of mental health as we explore topics such as self-love, loss, goal setting, gratitude, and more.

I know how stressful life can seem. I know what it feels like to be depressed and at my lowest point, not wanting to move forward. No longer will we neglect the importance of mental health. And so this book is for anyone who has ever felt alone, who knows what it's like to be at their lowest point, and is looking to grow, love themselves more, and live a more positive life. This book is for you.

# CHAPTER 1

# LOST

—

*"Not until we are lost do we begin to understand ourselves."*
—HENRY DAVID THOREAU

I never truly understood the meaning of Thoreau's words until my freshman year of college.

I just knew when I left high school that college was going to be a breeze. From what I had heard and seen in movies, college was all about partying and enjoying the best four years of your life. I had just been accepted into Georgetown University when I thought to myself, *I'll do my four years, get all As, graduate, and get my master's in two years with no problem.*

August 26 was move-in day. I arrived at my college dorm in Kennedy Hall, room 507. After carrying what felt like three tons of suitcases and a pack of fruit snacks, all my stuff was in my room. After taking a quick breather, my parents and I went shopping for a few essential items I'd need for the year before we said our goodbyes.

As they left, I soon reconnected with my old friend, anxiety—defined by Merriam-Webster's dictionary as "fear or nervousness about what might happen." I couldn't help but feel this emotion creeping up on me. I looked out the window to see the volleyball court and the Potomac river and wondered what this new transition and change in life would be like. I was over a thousand miles away from home. I had never been away on my own, and this was my first real step into adulthood. *What will the classes be like? I don't know anyone here. How will I make friends? Will people even like me?*

Class wouldn't start for another five days, but I had new student orientation (NSO) to look forward to. At NSO, I met everyone in my orientation advisor (OA) group as we were subjected to countless icebreakers throughout the day, what must have been a hazing ritual for the incoming freshmen that year. As we began walking around campus and learning about Georgetown, I did my best to make small talk with other students in my group.

I had a lot of fun over the course of the next few days. My OA group and I explored Chinatown in downtown DC. I got to ride a mechanical bull for the first time ever, and the last night of freshmen activities ended with free tacos from a taco truck. Looking back, I wish I would have savored all of those NSO moments longer. If I knew then what I know now, maybe I would have.

Wednesday, August 31, I woke up, got ready, took a mirror selfie to commemorate the day, and headed out to take on my first day of classes as an undergraduate student. As I boarded the elevator, I could feel the nervousness inside me rising as I didn't know what to expect from my first day.

It honestly wasn't as bad as I thought it'd be. The entire day was just professor introductions, reviewing syllabi, and being told to buy books I definitely couldn't afford. My jaw hit the floor when I browsed the campus bookstore for the recommended readings on each of my syllabi. Who had all this extra money just lying around after already paying so much in tuition?

Mid faint, I thought of something that would easily save me hundreds of dollars each semester. I went to my bittersweet frenemy, the place most of my classmates would study, sleep, eat, repeat, and call home over the years—the library. I looked up all of the books I needed for my classes and checked them out. From there, I simply renewed them every three weeks or so. Problem solved. My wallet and I were both relieved.

Now it was time to put something in my stomach before my next class. I headed to Leo's dining hall. I surveyed every station of the cafeteria for options, and I didn't see anything that really made my taste buds excited. There definitely wasn't anything like the home-cooked meals I was used to. I went downstairs and discovered ol' reliable—french fries! I paired it with a few other items and found a table where I sat and ate by myself before I made my way off to the rest of my classes.

Upon finishing and being drained from my last class, I headed back to the dining hall to grab dinner. It was packed with a herd of people standing at every station. I ate the same thing I had eaten at lunch and this time added some ice cream to go with it.

I headed back to my dorm and went to chill on my phone before getting a call from my mom. I was the first of her three boys to go off to school, and in her eyes I was still her baby. She asked me how things were going and wanted to see how my first day went. I told her everything was good and that it was only my first day, so things hadn't really picked up. After hanging up, I got ready for bed, tired from the long day.

I was officially a college student and couldn't wait to see what was in store for me next.

That first Friday night, I decided to walk the streets and see what a weekend at college was like. It was a new experience for me, but every party felt the same. I'd head inside, be offered a drink, lean against a grimy wall, and wait for a halfway decent song to come on so I could dance. At 2:00 a.m., I'd squeeze between people as I made my way out of the sweaty apartment. Tired and hungry, I'd make my way to the Epi's, one of the campus restaurants, for some soggy fries. They looked like I felt: soft, sad, and stale.

I repeated the same thing the next night, and before I knew it, it was already Sunday. It was as if the weekend had flown by. I hadn't done too much of anything besides going out, and now the school week was about to begin.

Over the next few weeks, I continued the same pattern. It seemed like the thing to do. It was a freedom like I had never had before, and with this freedom came unexpected consequences.

It was amazing how easy it was to get behind in my work. I wasn't too enthusiastic about going out, but it seemed like the only way to meet new people, and it surely beat staying in my dorm with nothing to do. I'd stay up all night, wake up late on Sundays, and begin my work late in the afternoon. This was my schedule, and each week it felt like I got more and more behind as the semester picked up.

On top of classes and my on-campus job, I decided to join pep band. I had been a percussionist since eighth grade, performing at different events throughout the city of Dallas for years. At my first practice, I quickly gravitated toward the best instrument there is—the quints drum. Five drums each with a different sound were sure to add some flavor. Even quicker than I had found my drum, I soon discovered how mundane the pep band was. I'd make suggestions on how we could be better, but we were only ever allowed to play the same songs over and over again. And like all of my classes, I usually had the most melanin in the room.

Not even a month in, the thrill of college and what I expected it to be had worn off. Not only was I not getting all As, but all of my classes were taking turns beating me up. I laughed at how naive I was for believing college would be a breeze. Being at such a prestigious school with unrealistic expectations being placed on me everywhere I looked only created a more stressful environment. Day in and day out, my insecurities paid me a visit:

*I'm not good enough to be here.*

*I still don't even know what I want to do with my life.*

I lacked assurance and self-confidence, the definition of being lost. My overthinking led to feelings of inadequacy which only further translated to my work. My motivation and drive began to lag, and I almost gave up on doing my work, only doing enough to just get by.

Somehow I scraped by and finals came around. After walking out the door of my last exam, I breathed a sigh of relief that it was all over. I had survived my first semester of college. It was nothing like what I expected or wanted it to be. It seemed that nothing had gone the way I planned.

If this was how my four years were going to go, I was in trouble.

As I was writing this book, I was curious to find someone who could relate to me and my experiences. I went looking for clarity in someone else, and then I met Dr. Jo Ellyn Walker. Like myself, Dr. Walker, a full-time counseling and psychiatric services (CAPS) psychologist at Georgetown University, found herself lost in school. As a first-generation college student at Northwestern University, she could not turn to her family and other people close to her for a good number of questions, so she had to figure things out on her own.

YOU'RE MORE THAN ENOUGH!

Her first issues began around midterms of her freshman year. She had a project where she had to come up with a story, research, and interview people, but nothing was going as planned.

"I just kept hitting dead ends, and the deadline was getting closer. I didn't know what to do."

She didn't feel comfortable going to the professor to ask for an extension for fear her professor would think she waited until the last minute. She had just accepted she was going to fail this assignment and would try to use the rest of her time to boost her grade enough to pass.

She expressed her frustration to a friend who suggested she ask for an extension or at least go talk with the professor and see what they would say. Dr. Walker was apprehensive about the idea but eventually ended up asking.

She emailed her professor explaining her situation and was pleasantly met with understanding, advice, and the extension.

"I was very surprised because I just didn't see that as an option. The old saying really rang true that closed mouths don't get fed… no one knew what I was going through because I didn't say anything."

Even a few years later as she looked across the graduation stage, she could still remember what it was like feeling lost in the world and hitting dead end after dead end.

"But through everything, I made it! It was actually pretty exciting being the first person in my family to graduate," Dr. Walker cheerfully recalls.

## YOU'RE WORTH IT! TIPS

### TIP #1: IT'S OKAY TO START OFF LOST

I shared both of these stories to show you that what you're going through is common. Whether it's myself, Dr. Walker, or even you, everyone at one point in their life has been lost. I didn't always feel like I was enough. I didn't know my purpose, and I didn't know where I belonged in the world. I discovered that while being lost takes you outside of your comfort zone, it also leads you to new paths, forcing you to face challenges that result in personal growth.

### TIP #2: KEEP PERSPECTIVE

Overthinking is one of the biggest causes of our unhappiness and gets us nowhere. That's why it's important to keep perspective. Many people feel like they're alone or like they're the only ones who are lost in life. This isn't the case. According to CNBC Make It, 51 percent of young Americans say they feel down, depressed, or hopeless.

As humans, we all experience disappointment but also joy, happiness, and laughter. I think it's a lot harder to make the connection to the positive when we feel like we constantly mess up or can't get anything right. Keeping perspective means knowing that it's perfectly acceptable to make mistakes. Use mistakes as an opportunity to learn rather than penalize or beat yourself up over every little thing.

Keeping perspective also means understanding you're not the only one who has ever gone through what you're going through. You're not the only person who may feel lost, and this feeling doesn't last forever. Everyone has their own kind of timing and journey, and you will find your path.

### TIP #3: SPEAK UP

As I spoke with Dr. Walker, she mentioned that even now as she provides counseling to students, she hears a lot of them say they feel like they need to figure everything out on their own. A recurring theme throughout my life I wish I had realized sooner is knowing it's more than okay to ask for help. Your internal struggle doesn't have to be fought alone. When it comes to your mental health, asking for help is one of the bravest things you can do; it doesn't make you appear weak or pathetic. It actually shows the love and care you have for yourself and how you want better than your current situation.

### TIP #4: COMBAT YOUR ANXIETY

"When you're feeling anxious, your thoughts race and you may start taking rapid, shallow breaths that come directly from the chest. This type of breathing, called thoracic or chest breathing, causes an upset in the oxygen and carbon dioxide levels in the body resulting in increased heart rate, dizziness, muscle tension, and other physical sensations. Your blood is not being properly oxygenated and this may signal a stress response that contributes to anxiety and panic attacks.

"Diaphragmatic or deep breathing, on the other hand, stimulates the parasympathetic nervous system, which is part of the peripheral nervous system responsible for regulating heartbeat, blood flow, breathing, and digestion. Deep breathing helps you to avoid the 'fight-or-flight' response (acute stress response) to mentally or physically terrifying situations" (VeryWell Mind).

1. Keeping your eyes open or closed, inhale through your nose while keeping your mouth shut. Hold it for three seconds and then exhale from your mouth for three seconds. You should hear yourself blowing all the air out as you release the built-up tension. Do this exercise in sets of ten, and continue to repeat it for several minutes until you feel more relaxed.

2. "Find your 'happy place.' Painting a mental picture of a place that makes you feel relaxed can actually calm your brain and body. When you start to feel anxious, sit in a quiet and comfortable place. Think of your ideal place to relax. While it can be any place in the world, real or imaginary, it should be an image that you find very calming, happy, peaceful, and safe. Make sure it's easy enough to think about so you can return to it in your mind when you feel anxious in the future. Think of all the small details you'd find if you were there. Think about how the place would smell, feel, and sound. Envision yourself in that place, enjoying it comfortably. Once you have a

good picture of your 'happy place,' close your eyes and take slow and regular breaths through your nose and out of your mouth. Be aware of your breathing and continue focusing on the place you've imagined in your mind until you feel your anxiety lifting. Visit this place in your mind whenever you feel anxious" (Healthline).

3. Combine exercises 1 and 2 above.

> *"Some beautiful paths can't be discovered*
> *without getting lost."*
> —EROL OZAN

———

## CHAPTER AFFIRMATION

At the end of each chapter, I will be including an affirmation. Affirmations are easily one of the biggest and most impactful game changers I started implementing into my life. They're a form of positive self-talk, usually in the form of short and simple statements or declarations. According to Healthline. com, "Affirmations can help strengthen self-worth by boosting both your positive opinion of yourself and your confidence in your ability to achieve your goals. They can also help counter the feelings of panic, stress, and self-doubt that often accompany anxiety."

It's amazing how these encouraging phrases can help combat negative thoughts, boost your self-esteem, empower you, and improve your mood while allowing you to take back control of your thoughts. Dr. Joseph Dispenza, a researcher, lecturer, and author who holds postgraduate training in the fields of neuroscience and neuroplasticity, quantitative electroencephalogram measurements (also known as brain mapping), mind–body medicine, and brain-heart coherence, explains that "our thoughts have a direct connection to our direct level of health. Thoughts make a chemical. If you have happy thoughts, then you're producing chemicals that make you feel happy."

To begin, write your affirmations down in your phone, in a journal, or on sticky notes. If you're writing them on sticky notes, place them on your mirror and around your room. Now that you have your affirmations written out, recite them aloud at least twice a day—when you first get up and right before bed. The more times you hear it, the more likely you'll believe as you alter your subconscious thoughts.

So rather than saying, "I feel so lost," consider adopting an affirmation such as…

"I know my story is not over yet!"

# WRITE YOUR OWN AFFIRMATIONS

Examples:

- I know I can accomplish anything I set my mind to!
- I believe in, trust, and have confidence in myself!
- I never give up!
- I turn obstacles into learning opportunities!

Now you give it a try and write a few of your own:

- I am _____

  _____!

- I will _____

  _____!

- I believe _____

  _____!

# RESOURCES

United States National Suicide Prevention Lifeline
(1-800-273-8255) or *https://SuicidePreventionLifeline.org*

The National Suicide Prevention Lifeline provides free and confidential emotional support to people in suicidal crisis or emotional distress twenty-four hours a day, seven days a week, across the United States. The lifeline is comprised of a national network of over 180 local crisis centers, combining custom local care and resources with national standards and best practices.

The Substance Abuse and Mental Health Services Administration's National Helpline 1-800-662-HELP (4357) or *https://www.SAMHSA.gov*

The SAMHSA Helpline is a free, confidential, 24/7, 365-day-a-year treatment referral and information service (in English and Spanish) for individuals and families facing mental or substance use disorders.

# CHAPTER 2

# ALWAYS & FOREVER

---

*"If you have the ability to love, love yourself first."*
—CHARLES BUKOWSKI

My sophomore year at Georgetown was one of the most peculiar years of my life.

The year started like any other. I had a full load of five classes and not a lot of free time. If I wasn't in class, you could usually find me somewhere getting food.

That's where the recruiter for the date auction found me.

During the time I'd been at Georgetown, the annual charity date auction was one of the biggest fundraisers each year—a place where people can place bids to win dates with someone and the funds go toward a good cause. Contestants would come out to a song, dance, recite a poem, or show off a talent, and the bids would begin. The atmosphere was always loud, thrilling, and rowdy. It was meant to be a night of fun... until I was asked to be in it.

While waiting in line to get our orders from Bull Dog Tavern, one of the restaurants on campus, a group of guys and I were approached by the "recruiter" of the date auction planning committee.

"Hey! I'm Symone with the Caribbean Culture Circle, and we could really use some help. We've been planning this date auction for months, and we still need a couple of guys to join in on the action. Would any of you be interested?"

"Oh, nah, that's not my scene," one of the guys said. "But why don't you ask Tre'?" He laughed and nudged me.

I looked up from my phone, bewildered. *What did he just suggest she ask me?*

Before I could even lock my screen, the girl was standing in front of me, batting her eyes in my face. "So how about it?"

"I don't think…"

"Please!" she begged. "We really need some more guys."

I looked down at her and sighed. My buddies were practically falling over with laughter as my nervousness began to expose itself. They knew this would make me uncomfortable. "Sure."

Everyone froze. "You mean it?" the recruiter asked. I hesitantly nodded my head.

She smiled and thanked me, leaving me waiting for my food and questioning what I had just gotten myself into.

A week before the event, all the participants had our first practice as a group. We were asked to each line up and walk one by one out the door to a song of our choice with our "sexiest walks." I did my best to walk out to "Ego (Remix)" by Beyoncé featuring Kanye West.

A complete failure.

I felt so uncomfortable just having those ten to fifteen people watch as I tried to figure out what I would do. I didn't have any real talents that I could display on command in front of others, the whole "sexy walk" thing wasn't my thing, and don't even get me started on my dancing. Like parallel parking, the worst part is always the witnesses. It was too late to back out, but again I wondered what I had gotten myself into.

The day of the date auction finally came. I had changed my song choice just a few days prior to "Planez" by Jeremih featuring J. Cole. The plan was to walk out to my song, take off my suit jacket and shirt, dance a little, receive a bid, and get the hell out of there.

I nervously walked to the student center. Once the event was about to begin, all the contestants lined up. I peeked inside the packed room, and my stomach dropped to my toes.

*That's a lot of people.*

My thoughts started racing uncontrollably. *What if no one places a bid on me? What will I do? I'm going to be embarrassed in front of everybody!*

I called one of my best friends, Isaac, who was already in the room waiting.

"Bro, I can't do this. You gotta bid on me if no one else does or at least ask one of the girls beside you. I'm begging you. I'll even pay you back after with interest."

Isaac laughed. "You'll be fine."

Click. In true friend fashion, he had hung up on me.

I didn't believe him when he said I'd be fine, but I had no other choice.

Four girls were set to go before me. One after the other, they boldly went into the room, and I was up next. Quick gasps left my body. I took a deep breath as the music started, and I walked through the doors and began. Everywhere I looked, I saw flashing lights, but I made sure to avoid direct eye contact with anyone. I slowly unbuttoned my jacket and tossed it into the crowd. Lip syncing with every lyric, I then went for my shirt next. I heard screams, but I was doing my best to block out everything. I ended my performance and, with that, the bidding began. Awkward silence at first, almost as awkward as I felt during my entire entrance with all those eyes on me as I made my way to the front of the room.

We waited like that for what felt like an eternity. Then a bid came in. My heart practically stopped. I wasn't sure if it was a pity bid or what, but I appreciated the lifeline.

A second and final bid came from another woman, someone I had never seen before. *Someone had bid on me?* I couldn't believe it. When the bidding was closed, I hurried backstage to get changed.

The rest of the show went by like a blur. As everyone was leaving, I found Isaac and asked him to point out the girl who had placed the winning bid on me. When we finally found her, my heart stopped. She was beautiful. I could tell she was not like any of the other women I had ever met. She carried herself differently. All the embarrassment and nervousness I had felt was worth this moment. At the end of the night, I walked her to the front gates and watched her get in her Uber.

The next day, I was out with my boys when she called me and told me she was back on campus for an event. Just like that, I was off to see her. Two days later, I went to her campus—the first of many times—to study. From there, we'd text and talk all day, every day. Just getting that notification put a smile on my face.

I had found happiness like I had never known before. She was the best part of my entire year and really the entire time since I had been in college. She made my life at the time a lot more tolerable and was the only thing that made me happy. Good times, shared laughs, her voice, her mannerisms, our inside jokes, having someone to talk to about anything, someone who kept me from my loneliness, everything.

A couple months into our relationship, I decided to surprise her by showing up to her favorite event of the season, Maryland Day—the University of Maryland's annual celebration with dance performances, food, bounce houses, music, and entertainment. I'll never forget the look on her face when she saw me. It was everything I had hoped for and more. She took me by the hand and introduced me to her family. We spent the day together just like that and, by the end of the night, I knew I was ready to tell her why I had come out all this way.

"I love you," I said, tracing the pattern of her bed with my finger.

She laughed. "You know, I was just thinking to myself that this boy must really love me to come out all this way. I love you too."

I had never experienced love before or even thought too much about it, but in that moment I just knew this is what love must be. She was my happiness. I loved her more than anything else in the world—including myself.

Though my feelings for her never changed, our circumstances did as I spent the fall semester back home in Texas.

We thought we could make it work.

After a couple of months, things started to take a turn for the worse and ultimately fell apart. Our conversations grew shorter, more tense. We started getting into petty arguments over every little thing. The distance, misunderstandings, blame game of who was right who was wrong: It was like trying to fix things only made everything worse. Eventually, these small arguments grew bigger and bigger until our differences became insurmountable. She broke up with me right before I was to about to return back to Georgetown's campus.

I'd go sit in my car a few times a week, contemplating my whole life, yelling and screaming out in frustration. And I'd cry tears of anger and hurt wondering why I was so misunderstood.

I was devastated. I couldn't believe it. Why was this happening? What had happened to us? Why couldn't we work through this like we always did? She was my rock, my everything. Without her, what did I have left? I was afraid of being alone again and once more felt like my life wasn't going anywhere.

I felt like I was spinning my wheels but couldn't get traction. I spent countless nights obsessing over where things had gone wrong and how we could get back to where we were before. I couldn't let it go. Not now. Not during the worst year of my life. I tried calling her a million times only to realize my number was blocked. I thought if I could just apologize, everything would be better, *that we would be better.* I couldn't give her up. She was my person. But it was over.

*What a great way to start the new year,* I thought, *losing everything that mattered to me, the one person I would've done anything and everything for.* I had not only lost my partner, but my best friend; they don't tell you that part. I was at my lowest point. This was my rock bottom.

YOU'RE STRONGER THAN WHAT YOU'RE GOING THROUGH!

So during the day I'd go to class, and at night I'd look at the ceiling as my tears flooded my pillow again and again, praying for my only escape—sleep. It never came quick enough, and the memories haunted me and replayed in my mind every day. I would wipe away my tears, but it was useless. The more I remembered, the more I cried. It sucked being hurt and physically hurt even more knowing that someone I loved held me responsible for their hurt.

The depression consumed me, and I was no longer me. I was tired of everything. Food. Music. Life. I had never experienced this much pain. I didn't know what the point of anything was.

Even surrounded by all those people on campus, I felt alone. I remained tucked away in the comfort of my hoodie. No one saw me. I took different routes to class to see fewer people, put on fake smiles, and ate at different times whenever I did actually force myself to eat. I would rarely smile, and when I did I could feel the blank empty stare in my eyes. I was broken inside. For months, I stayed trapped in my thoughts, and no one knew what I was going through. I wrongfully kept it to myself. Deep down inside I was suffering, and ironically I was still able to instill positivity and happiness and inspiration in others. I finished the semester doing well in my classes and did what I needed to do, but there wasn't too much to celebrate.

All that I loved was no longer in my life.

# YOU'RE WORTH IT! TIPS

Heartbreak and breakups are never easy, and, if I'm being honest with you, there's no one-size-fits-all way of fixing a broken heart. I was literally at my lowest point in life after this, but I want to offer you some tips where you can be better than me and overcome.

## TIP #1: DON'T IDEALIZE YOUR EX

I watched an interesting TED talk by psychologist Guy Winch in which he talked about how to fix a broken heart. He warns against idealizing your ex instead of focusing on how wrong they were for you. "To avoid idealizing, you have to balance them out by remembering their frown not just their smile and how bad they made you feel... compile a list of all the ways the person was wrong for you, all the bad qualities, all the pet peeves, and then keep it on your phone. If you want to get over them, you have to remind yourself frequently that they weren't perfect and neither was the relationship," he states. I used to daydream about my ex-girlfriend—when I would see her again, replaying everything back through my mind over and over again searching for a "why." This hope only further set me back until I realized it was time to accept that it was over and let go.

## TIP #2: MAKE A LIST OF THE IDEAL PERSON FOR YOU

I reached out and spoke with Meleena Phillips, author of *The Shameful Casualties of Love*. As someone who writes about tackling the consequences of unhealthy romantic relationships, I was curious to hear her thoughts.

My biggest takeaway from our conversation was to define and lay out what type of person you're looking for in your life. This lines up exactly with what Guy Winch says as well. I like the fact that Meleena lays out the importance of knowing what you want out of any relationship while normalizing that you don't need another person to be whole or in control of your life. I feel like that's something I struggled with myself—putting my source of happiness into someone else.

So when you go about finding that "perfect" individual, and that feeling later dissipates or goes away, now you're in a place of feeling lost. You don't know yourself or who you are because you put so much into this other person rather than putting it into yourself.

Choose yourself, and pour all of the love and energy you would into someone else into yourself first. Be the source of your own happiness, and any relationship (friendships, romantic, or otherwise) should add value and happiness to your life—not be the source of it. I wasn't able to help myself until I took the time to truly get to know who I was.

### TIP #3: SOCIAL SUPPORT

For me, spending time with my friends helped me heal my broken heart. For you, some time with your family may be just the thing you need to start to feel whole again. Find your people—the ones who make you laugh until milk comes out of your nose and who are willing to stay up late with you to talk on the phone about nothing.

I realized the only way to get past my breakup was to fill the void and my time with other things that made me happy. Whether I'm experiencing heartbreak or anything else, I try to find a reason to laugh and smile every day. I love comedy and stand-ups as they transport me to another place and the laughter removes my pain. It's such a great and much-needed break from feeling down all the time. I even put together a "Funny" playlist on YouTube of all my favorite segments, stand-ups, things that make me laugh, and things I want to check out that I know will make me smile.

Every time I want to unwind or get my mind off of things and have a good time, I click one of the videos and watch it. I understand I have to be patient with myself and that part of healing is self-care. So I actively took and take the steps to do that for myself, even if that means putting everything else on pause to watch Bernie Mac, Richard Pryor, Jamie Foxx, Eddie Griffin, the 85 South Show, and all the other legendary comedians.

## TIP #4: TAKE TIME TO HEAL

With time, I was able to accept my past without letting it control me. I won't lie to you: It took a good amount of time for the pain of our breakup to subside, but I realized a few things that really helped. One of the biggest takeaways is accepting how you feel and taking the time to truly heal. You can't ignore a broken heart.

FIND A REASON TO LAUGH AND SMILE EVERY DAY!

After a while, the pain of our breakup started to pass. Memories of our time together were no longer at the forefront of my mind. As time goes on, after you've accepted how you feel rather than internalize your feelings, a weight is lifted off your shoulders.

For the first time in a long time, I started to like and become comfortable with my own company. I didn't need her to feel whole. Every now and then, I'd remind myself that I may be damaged at times, but I am not broken. Yes, you may have scars, but you also can and will rebuild.

After my heartbreak, I had felt more undesired, rejected, alone, and misunderstood—as if the entire world had given up on me. It's important to learn from every experience, good or bad, in life. Loss hurts us all, but better days are always coming. I knew I deserved and wanted better for myself, and you do too.

Know that your value is more than one relationship. Your life doesn't end when someone walks out of it. Just because your flame may go dim from time to time doesn't mean it has to go out. You will heal.

*"Accept what is, let go of what was, and have faith in what will be."*

—SONIA RICOTTI

———

## CHAPTER AFFIRMATION

I will love myself first, always and forever!

# CHAPTER 3

# CHANGING
# THE NARRATIVE

———

*"To live in hearts we leave behind is not to die."*
—THOMAS CAMPBELL

There are other forms of loss that we can experience besides heartbreak. One of my close friends, Lamont, has lived one full life. He was born in Miami, Florida, specifically Liberty City, one of the most dangerous hoods in the country. Lamont learned the meaning of death and grief from a very young age.

He was maybe seven years old the first time he saw life being taken away. He and his older brother had just come back to their apartment complex one Friday evening. In the apartment complex where he stayed, there was a wall that divided the complexes. Before they came upstairs, they saw three guys dressed in all black. Lamont knew something was off as it wasn't typical for anyone to be hanging by the wall that led to the parking lot in the back of the apartments. They ran up the stairs and watched the guys from their bedroom window.

It was almost 10:00 p.m. when the resident who lived there showed up. As the man was getting ready to enter his place, they laid low behind the wall. Once the door was unlocked, they jumped the wall and ran up behind him. It was a home invasion.

"Everything just happened so fast." The man was caught off guard and tried to put up a fight before gunshots rang out. "I saw his body drop. From my window, me and my brother witnessed it right then, right there." The guy didn't even fully get past the doorsteps of his apartment.

"It was just so crazy to me, but it was normal too. Moving forward, I definitely started seeing the world through a different lens. I'm sad to say I've seen those things happen over and over."

Football was his ticket out. "Sports saved my life in a lot of ways. It kept me from being involved and following my peers, who were doing all the wrong things at the time period, because I wanted more to be involved and active in sports." So every day, Lamont either had to train or go to practice, the type of activities that didn't allow him to put himself in a predicament where he would either lose his freedom or life at a young age.

He was really trying to go to the NFL because he felt he possessed the talent to make it that far. "School was more of an escape from that world I knew, and sports kept me out of trouble. I'd go to school throughout the day, practice, do training, come home, and eat. By the time I came home, I was too tired to even try to go out and do anything else. And so it kind of kept me out of trouble, and it kept me alive."

Playing sports was that safe haven for Lamont all the way up until college, at which point he felt like the system had further failed him. He was given an opportunity to go to college— University of Florida—but he was declared ineligible on the day it was time to go to school. The NCAA declared him ineligible because they said he cheated on his test scores due to his high school GPA not matching his test scores. Lamont just couldn't catch a break.

Essentially, because his GPA was so low, it was not possible he was able to test that high, combined with his poor performance on his first SAT.

"I took my first SAT on the day after a football game. I got in real late because the game had been pushed back due to thunderstorms. So I got in in the a.m. and then had to wake right back up at five or six just to get to the testing center in a timely fashion. I fell asleep on my first test and didn't even finish it. So with my GPA and with me falling asleep on my first test, they assessed that it couldn't have been me who took the second test. That system really pissed me off. My mentality at the time was 'Y'all don't really want me to be here at school, so forget that.' I can go over to the streets and get money because it was easier."

The ineligibility was a serious roadblock for Lamont. He was already teetering the fence, going back and forth, and with that taking place he just jumped the fence and chose to take the route of the streets.

"I made good money but lost loved ones, friends. When you look at it from living a lifestyle, you know, it was nice. The road was a roller coaster ride. I mean, losing money came with the territory as part of the game. So when I lost money, I didn't worry about it too much. Now, no one is happy about the fact of losing money. But then, with that street mentality, I just looked at it as all fails, and any and everything will prevail. But losing friends, especially my best friend from childhood, was my lowest point."

Shaun Juan is what everyone called Lamont's best friend. He favored Busta Rhymes a lot, as if they could've been twins, especially when Busta had dreads. One day, Lamont had just made it to his block, his hood, on 15th Avenue when he got a call from Shaun.

"Wassup bro? I need you to come pick me up," said Shaun.

"I gotchu. I'll be there in a little bit," replied Lamont.

Lamont was there holding a conversation with friends, and before he knew it he noticed a helicopter up in the sky. And it was hovering in the vicinity of where Shaun stays, not too far from where he had to go pick him up from.

"Ay, Lamont, they just shot and killed Busta Rhymes!" a guy yelled from his car as he pulled up.

"They killed Busta Rhymes, the rapper?" Lamont asked confused.

"Nah, man. Ya boy, Busta... what's his name? Shaun!"

Lamont looked up again at the helicopter and immediately took off and rolled over there. When he got to the house, he saw the young woman who had just lost the father of her child. She was crying on the steps a few feet away from where Shaun had just been shot.

"The body wasn't covered or anything. Seeing him like that was the most devastating moment in my life. Me and him, we was like every day, every morning, every night just hanging out. Wake up in the morning, boom, he hit me up. When I wake up, I call him. When he wake up, he called me. Every day you saw us together. So losing him... yeah, it was a crazy moment. That was a low point."

That was everyday life in some sense for Lamont, but it hit even harder when it happened to that one person who's like family, like a brother, to him. A loss like this can bring about an intense feeling of loneliness, depression, pain, and anger.

"It comes with the territory. Today you could be here, tomorrow you could be gone. When you live an abnormal life, you find it acceptable that any can be your last day. And that's a man with no plan, truth be told. Yeah, you may have a plan to survive out there within those streets, but you don't truly have a plan for life when it comes to looking to create that generational wealth or establish the legacy for your family or just for yourself. Living that life, you really don't think that far. You just live in that moment."

It's normal during times like these to feel isolated, to breakdown, and to cry for hours on end.

"I didn't know how I would continue on in the world alone. I just was in disbelief. Even with this being everyday life in some sense, man, I cried like a baby the next day or two."

## YOU'RE WORTH IT! TIPS

### TIP #1: SURROUND YOURSELF WITH LOVED ONES

Losing someone is never easy. In times of loss and grief, it's easy to feel completely alone. Surrounding yourself with those who care about you can help with your grieving and healing process. There is no one-size-fits-all way to grieve as everyone grieves differently, but it's important not to hide your true feelings. "Grieving can be an emotional rollercoaster, and it helps to be surrounded by loved ones who are there for you. It's okay to talk about how your loved one died as repeating the story is a way of processing and accepting the death" (HelpGuide). Remember that there is no time limit on your healing, so take the all the time you need to grieve.

## TIP #2: THEY WILL NOT BE FORGOTTEN

The bond of love is not broken by death, and your love for them will surely outlast any period of grief. You will encounter difficult days, but they won't last forever. What does last forever are the memories of them you hold, the good times you shared, each time you made one another smile, and your favorite phone calls. Let these memories act as comfort for you, and share their stories of what they meant to you.

## TIP #3: TIGHT HUGS

The people you hold near and dear are part of what makes life great. So for those still physically in your life, make sure you show them how much they mean to you. Send them a quick text to ask how they're doing and let know that you were thinking about them. Visit them. Pick up the phone and check in on your family and friends; you never know what someone else is going through and how much of a difference the sound of your voice can make. Enjoy every moment you get with those you love and the genuine individuals who support and uplift you. If talking and verbally expressing your emotions isn't your greatest strength, write them a thoughtful letter on why you appreciate them in your life. And every chance you get, hug them and hold them as tightly as possible.

ENERGY NEVER DIES!

## TIP #4: CREATE A LIFE FOR YOURSELF THEY'D BE PROUD OF

It's true that energy never dies, and it's up to us to carry the energy of those we love and embody the best parts of them. Lamont's story never stopped with the loss of his best friend because his best friend is always with him. Those you have lost are now part of you and live on through you. Lamont and Shaun knew each other since they were twelve years old. They went to school at Central High together. One of Shaun's best qualities was that he was a laid back, chill, smart individual. He was a thinking man. He had a true hustler's mentality. As they hung out on a day-to-day basis, Lamont recognized certain qualities about him that he found inspiring and picked those habits and qualities up himself. Even with all the death, loss, and countless obstacles, Lamont continues to push forward and do great things in life, including his recent graduation from Georgetown University.

"It's easy to lay down. It's easy to stop, lay down, and quit, but is it rewarding if you take the easy route? So when I think about that, when I think of the people who have achieved great accomplishments, when I think about the game changers—the Martin Luther Kings, the Michael Jordans—when I just think of their story, nothing about their story was easy; nothing about their achievements were easy. So when I paid attention to those things, I realized for myself that nothing's going to stop me from striving to achieve greatness. When my boys from the block look at me, they see there's a better path instead of the streets, and they see I'm changing the narrative in my life for me and for Shaun!"

*"What we once enjoyed and deeply loved we can never lose,
for all that we love deeply becomes part of us."*
—HELEN KELLER

---

## CHAPTER AFFIRMATION

I am healing!

## RESOURCES

*www.HelpGuide.org/Articles/Grief/
Coping-With-Grief-And-Loss.htm*

HelpGuide is a small, independent nonprofit that runs one of
the world's top ten mental health websites. Over fifty million
people from all around the world turn to HelpGuide each
year for trustworthy content they can use to improve their
mental health and make healthy changes. As I was doing
research for this book and this chapter specifically, I came
across their website and wanted to share this great resource
with you.

# CHAPTER 4

# OVERCOME

---

*"Strength doesn't come from what you can do. It comes from overcoming the things you once thought you couldn't."*
—RIKKI ROGERS

Growing up, I was always very risk averse. I was known as Mr. Picky Eater. "Oh no, he doesn't eat that. Oh no, he doesn't eat that, either," or "Oh, he doesn't like that." I would never try any new foods because I was always afraid I wouldn't like them.

When I was a kid, my mom would always force me to eat black-eyed peas. She knew I couldn't stand black-eyed peas. I'd get my plate of food and immediately spot the outsider which didn't belong. A confused look would come across my face. *She knows I don't like black-eyed peas, so why would she put some on my plate?* I'd eat around it. Cornbread? I love bread, so no problem. Grilled chicken with gravy on top? Absolutely, sign me up for seconds. Freshly warmed white rice with sugar mixed? Oh, baby. And at the end of my lavish and cheerful feast came the uninvited party guest. My mom would catch me every time I tried to sneak off. I'd pretend to be full, and she'd say, "You better eat them black-eyed peas. You are not allowed to leave that dinner table until you do!" And the black-eyed peas and I would stare each other down, neither of us wanting to concede, until my mother would literally force feed them to me ruining what should've been a beautiful meal.

This carried into my teenage years. I would never go out to parties in high school because I was always afraid of what could possibly happen. I never traveled or went anywhere. If it didn't involve food, school, church, or the barbershop, I simply wasn't going. It just wasn't for me. I lived in a little safety net of my own, where I didn't explore or try and do things. I was always afraid of what could happen. "Well what if this?" or "What if that?" I thought of worst case scenarios when it came to life, and that kept me in my bubble.

The first real step I took against this didn't come until I was nineteen years old when my family and I decided to go on a cruise. Taking a break from my overwhelmed summer that year, I prepared to fly home from DC for the much-needed trip. I had never been on a cruise or traveled outside of the country before, but I did want to have this experience with my family.

My mom and brother called me a few weeks before we left so we could plan out every minute of our cruise. I nodded along to their suggestions, happy for the distraction from my coursework, until my brother asked something that made the hair on my arm stand up.

"What about ziplining?"

My mom laughed. "That sounds like fun! Tre', what do you think?"

*Hell no,* I thought to myself. *Nope. No way. Nuh-uh. No.*

My brain was going a mile a minute. Ziplining was too dangerous for me. What if I broke a leg? What if I died?

But also, what if I missed out on an amazing memory with my family?

My heart stood still. I was tired of being afraid, tired of rationalizing my way out of new experiences. It was time to make a change. I knew I was at a place where I no longer wanted to let this fear of things, or really anything in life, control me. For years, I felt like I had been missing out on everything—on life.

"Sure," I choked.

It was set. I was in. My mom booked the tickets while we were on the phone. There was no going back.

My family and I piled into my mom's and aunt's vehicles and hit the road for Galveston. We could see our ship from miles out. My chest tightened. This was it. My first big trip. I couldn't tell if my heart was racing from anxiety or anticipation. Maybe it was a little of both.

YOU CAN DO IT!

When we were finally able to board, I couldn't believe my eyes. Light pop music blared from the ship's speakers as people milled about the halls between shops and activity rooms. Was this what I had been missing out on my whole life?

So my brothers, my cousin, and I explored the ship.

And we would go to a new place every few days. The first stop was Cozumel, Mexico, the second was the Cayman Islands, and the third was when we finally arrived to Jamaica.

The first thing we did when we got off the ship was check out some of the local shops and everything while we waited for our bus to take us to where the ziplining and tubing were. We drove about fifteen minutes to get there.

Our tour guides said, "Okay, this way for ziplining." So we began to line up for ziplining. They strapped the harness on me and buckled everything up. Of course, I had to check it a few times. We stopped at the edge of a bridge. All I saw was the top of huge trees with the leaves blowing in the wind. I was listening to the instructor speak, and as I looked down, my sense of hearing began to fail me.

*That's a long fall down*, I thought as I began writing my will in my head. We must've been at least twenty stories above what could've well been my final resting place.

"All right. Let's get started," the instructor said.

My breathing began to pick up. I found myself walking to the back. People started to go, and now it was my turn.

I finally stepped up, and it just seemed like my body didn't want to move. Everything I was seeing went against what I previously knew. Here I am on solid land, and you're telling me I'm supposed to just run off? You're telling me, "Hey, I want you to run off this bridge here. I know you can't fly, but I want you to run off with this and just trust the wire." *We clearly see with these eyes God gave us that the cliff ends right there.* I didn't think I'd be able to get my legs to move.

I had specifically come here to overcome this fear. My fear was internally asking me, "What are you doing? Why are you doing this? What if the line breaks?" But I was already at the platform and didn't want to hold anyone up. So I got "ready," grabbed the handle above, and began to run. I barely picked my feet up, and then suddenly I wasn't on solid land anymore.

My eyes were closed. My heart was pounding. I just wanted it to be over as quickly as possible.

I slowly opened my eyes as I felt the cool air brushing against my face.

The view was so beautiful that I forgot about my fear. I looked at the water below and the nature all around me as I flew in between the huge trees. I felt free, and it was one of the best feelings ever. I remember when I landed on the other side, all I could think was, *Let's do the next one!* This coming from the same guy who one minute ago was ready to turn around and head back to the cruise ship.

Fear was holding me captive from actually living life. Had I not been willing to try something new, I would have missed out on the joy of that amazing experience and not been able to overcome my fear. Before this, I felt confined to my comfort zone. But I felt free in the air and free mentally too. Because to me, fear leads to missing out on the best parts of life.

Fear keeps us from freedom.

## YOU'RE WORTH IT! TIPS

The biggest obstacles in life can be conquered once we overcome our mental hurdles. Fear and the expectation of something going wrong are often times far scarier than that which we believe we are afraid of. There have been countless times where I've psyched myself out about what may happen only to later realize and say to myself, "Oh, that wasn't even that bad."

This fear and overthinking are not uncommon to anyone, including Dr. Rolanda Findlay—a former naval aerospace experimental psychologist.

"Overthinking was my playground. That is where I would dwell. It was my Achilles heel," Dr. Findlay states.

In a job that requires a lot of critical thinking, she realized early in her career that thinking too much can actually be limiting in taking action and moving forward.

How do you combat this?

After brainstorming solutions, we came up with the following coping tools to help you battle your stress, anxiety, and fear when it comes to trying new things and simply navigating everyday life.

## TIP #1: JOURNAL

One of the biggest turning points in both of our lives came when we started journaling. Journaling is a critical tool because it allows you to take information that's circling in your brain in thinking mode and put it on paper. Journaling allows you to release these thoughts. Releasing that energy out of yourself and getting it onto another surface can take that pressure off. Writing it down also ensures you won't forget it and helps to process what you're thinking. You can also consider exploring other types of journaling like voice and video recordings.

## TIP #2: MEDITATE

Another powerful tool that helps with stepping back and stepping away is meditation. According to Verywell Mind, "Meditation has been shown to have a wide number of psychological, emotional, and health-related benefits such as better management of anxiety disorder and depression systems, better stress management skills, increased self-awareness, improved emotional well-being, and greater empathy for yourself and others."

It's something I didn't really start until my senior year of college as a way to practice mindfulness. Like breathing, one of the really cool things about meditation is that it's free and can be accessed right away. To begin, I'd wake up at the same time every day and find a quiet place (this was usually my room). Since I was new to this, I'd set a timer for five minutes before later moving it up to ten and fifteen minutes. After that, I'd find a comfortable spot either in my chair or sitting on the floor with my legs folded underneath my body and begin the same breathing exercises mentioned in chapter one.

As I breathed, I would let all of my thoughts come to the forefront—both good and bad. I'd focus on, acknowledge, and allow myself to actually feel what I was feeling in order to better understand my emotions. Lastly, I'd mentally focus on what I was going to accomplish each day and then go conquer the day.

### TIP #3: CHANGE YOUR ENVIRONMENT

Whether you've been staring at screens all day or you're in a tense meeting and feel the energy of "this is not it," make sure you change your environment. Step out of the room, go for a walk, stretch your legs, get some sunlight, and move your body. And if you really need a peaceful break, go find a body of water. Just admiring the beauty of nature and listening to the flow of the water is so calming.

## TIP #4: LISTEN TO MUSIC

Anxiety, fear of the unknown, and overthinking can certainly play a number on one's confidence, which is why it's something Dr. Findlay works on daily for herself. According to her, "Every day there's a daily example of having to face that dragon, but it becomes easier every day. The more it becomes a habit, the more I can kind of catch myself when I'm going into a spiraling loop and say, 'I am taking a step back,' and then I'll be good enough to get back to it."

Whenever we get trapped in a spiraling loop of anxiety and overthinking, it can help to listen to music. If you have music or a song that can transition you to another place, listen to it. Really it's about trying to bring your body and your energy from the space that it's currently in. You're trying to interrupt this loop and momentum of bad energy and bad thoughts. And you can interrupt it because you have all the tools you need to bring yourself back to a level space. I myself even have a "Smile/Hype" playlist on YouTube. It's made up of nothing but nostalgic songs and a list of my favorite tunes that get me hyped, make me smile, and remind me of great memories in my life.

## TIP #5: TAKE A SHOWER

This is an interesting one, but depending on how intense your anxiety is, taking a shower is one of those things that help interrupt it from running wild. If you're in your house and ruminating or perhaps replaying an incident that happened earlier in the day, sometimes changing clothes and going and taking that shower—things we might not even be thinking about—really help interrupt that negative process. A lot of times, it's the unknown that haunts us, but it's all in our heads. And a shower can help bring about more peace of mind.

### TIP #6: CREATE A MAX OUT LIST

I've never really liked the phrase "bucket list." It carries a negative connotation of having to do things before you kick the bucket. So, I created what I call a "max out" list.

A max out list or max fulfillment list is a list of things you want to do or try in your life. It's about maximizing your experiences, achieving your goals, and getting the most out of life. These can be things such as meeting Will Smith, visiting a certain country, writing a book, trying a new food, or learning to fly a plane.

The "fulfillment" part of max fulfillment comes from these actions and experiences adding fulfillment to your life. Not only is this a great way to try things you've never done, but it also gives you more ways to have fun and things to look forward to. Remember that dreams are meant to be fulfilled, and life is meant to be enjoyed!

> *"Too many of us are not living our dreams*
> *because we are living our fears."*
> —LES BROWN

**ENJOY LIFE!**

## CHAPTER AFFIRMATION

Fear is only a feeling, and it will not hold me back!

## WRITE YOUR OWN OBSTACLES TO OVERCOME

- I want to and will overcome _____

_____!

- I will no longer fear _____

_____!

- _____

_____ will no longer scare me!

- Fear can't keep me from _____

_____!

- Three things on my max out list are _____

_____

_____!

# CHAPTER 5

# BLESSINGS IN DISGUISE

---

*"Gratitude is a powerful catalyst for happiness. It's the spark
that lights a fire of joy in your soul."*

—AMY COLLETTE

It was spring of my sophomore year of high school, and I
had just stumbled upon a program called the Dallas Mayor's
Intern Fellows Program. As I read more about it, I saw it was
a program that offered students summer internships at major
companies throughout the city. Being the young ambitious
individual I was, I immediately went to apply.

Once I submitted my application, I was told that interested
companies would schedule an interview time for the upcom-
ing job fair in a few weeks. I spent several nerve-racking
days waiting by my inbox to hear back. Silence. After some
thoughtful consideration, I decided it was time to take matters into my own hands and check the portal. I held my
breath as I logged in to my account.

"We're sorry to inform you that no companies have scheduled
to interview with you at this time."

Disappointed, a blank stare fell over my face for a few seconds. "It's okay," I told myself. I knew the job fair was coming up, and that would be my chance to redeem myself. I figured the lack of an interview time would just give me the freedom to walk up and speak to whomever if they were available.

The night before the job fair, I walked into my parents' bedroom and asked them for tips on how to interview. This was my first ever interview; I mean, I was just barely sixteen years old. I stayed in the room with them for maybe an hour as they sat up in bed and relayed advice and suggestions on ways for me to stand out and make the best impression. Now that I actually knew what an interview was and what I was supposed to do at one, I had to get to bed because tomorrow was the big day!

I came to school the next day, dressed up in my suit and tie, with my mom's business briefcase. She had given it to me as I was making my way out the door as a way to carry the copies of my résumé with me. I walked downstairs to the main floor of my high school. The loud hallway was filled with both nervousness and excitement as everyone was preparing to load up the buses and head to the job fair.

Once we got there, I surveyed the room of over three hundred companies sitting at their booths. I stepped to the side to catch my breath. My parents had told me to just be myself and treat each interview as if I were having a regular conversation. I took a deep breath and walked up to my first booth.

"Hello, hello, my name is Tre' Bohannon. How are you?"

**KEEP MOVING FORWARD!**

"Nice to meet you, Tre'. I'm good. I really like your briefcase," said the interviewer.

Already off to a good start. *Maybe this won't be so bad, after all*, I thought to myself.

The more the conversation went on, the more the nervousness and uncertainty diminished. Things were going well just by being myself. At the end of that first interview, I shook the interviewer's hand with a smile on my face, ready to success-fully tackle the rest.

I ended the trip completing about six or seven interviews before my group was called to return to the buses. As I rode back to the school, I couldn't help but feel pretty accom-plished and proud of myself.

This accomplished feeling was confirmed a few days later when I received four different job offers. I couldn't help but smile in disbelief. *Wait till my parents hear about this!*

We evaluated each of the offers. I had always been business inclined, so I decided to accept the offer from one of the biggest banking institutions in the world. I was so excited to start my first real job; I felt on top of the world!

On my first day of work, I met my team and the other seven high school interns and got acquainted with where every-thing was, starting with the ping-pong table room. Things were going well that first week, but the excitement I had from my first day quickly diminished.

As my internship continued, I sensed the growing animosity from the woman I was assigned to work with, and the world came crashing down. She was mean every time I tried to help. She was bitter, tried to belittle me, and would make me copy mail for six to eight hours every day—not exactly how I imagined my first job to be.

Even when my program coordinator came to speak with her, he was met with the same rudeness. She didn't change, and each day seemed to come with some new form of torture. I kept telling myself it would be over soon. When my internship finally ended, I was so happy that I would never have to see or work with this individual ever again.

Today, whenever I reflect back on this job, I remember how much I hated it. And yet, I still look at it as one of the best things that ever happened to me. Toward the end of that internship, I had visited one of the other interns who also went to my school. While visiting him, the woman he was directly working with and I built a relationship. I was able to find solace in her as she instantly took me under her wing. She wrote my letter of recommendation that year, and to this day she is someone I consider a great friend and mentor. That terrible internship along with her letter of recommendation led to my next internship the next summer. That second internship led to a TV interview with the mayor of Dallas. Both internships and this interview allowed me to stand out and get accepted to Georgetown University.

I took an awful experience, used it as a means to my end (even though I didn't see it while I was going through it), and made it a part of my success story.

# YOU'RE WORTH IT! TIPS

## TIP #1: MAKE A GRATITUDE JOURNAL

The situation at my first job was nowhere near ideal nor what I imagined it to be. Times like that make it really hard to even want to think about being grateful for anything. It's so easy to get caught up in everything going on in the world that we often overlook the things we already have in our lives.

Complaining doesn't help you move forward or overcome what you're complaining about. But taking something positive from every situation and being in a state of gratitude will bring peace and allow you to appreciate the greater things in store for you. It's the little things in life now at this moment that make life what it truly is, and one of the best instruments that helped me see these things was creating and keeping a gratitude journal.

A gratitude journal is a journal or notebook that you use to write down the things in your life you are grateful for. Your gratitude journal can be the same journal that Dr. Findlay and I mentioned in the last chapter, or it can be its own separate journal.

I want to share a quick personal example of the positive impact my gratitude journal has had in helping me shift my mindset. Anyone in my family will be the first to tell you that I am not the biggest fan of washing dishes. Just the mention of someone asking me to wash them would make me say, "Ugh." I'd always think to myself, *Why can't someone else do them? Why do I have to wash dishes?*

While doing the dishes was and is still not my favorite thing in the world to do, my mindset has shifted from "having to" do the dishes to "getting to" do the dishes. The fact that I have dishes to wash means that I ate today. My family ate today. And that's something often overlooked but definitely worthy of being thankful for.

Food to eat, family, friends, a roof over your head, and the fact that breath still runs through your body are all things to be grateful for. We don't always realize how blessed we are or notice the things we "get to" do instead of "have to" do. Writing down what you're thankful for every day or each week can be a powerful tool in helping to appreciate life, expressing gratitude, and allowing you to start and operate each day with a more grateful heart. As you begin journaling, you start to notice things you didn't before. You see what and who matter to you most. It's now up to you to prioritize those individuals and things in your life.

### TIP #2: CELEBRATE YOUR SMALL WINS

Take the time to appreciate and notice your own progress and wins—no matter how small. You finished that course, you learned a new skill, you gave a speech for the first time, you tried something new, you lost five pounds, you beat your anxiety, you made it through a rough day, you're halfway through reading a great book. Whatever it is, show some gratitude to yourself. Take a moment to appreciate your strength and what you accomplished this week, because you deserve it.

## TIP #3: NEW DAY, NEW OPPORTUNITY

Someone recently asked me, "How are you?" I replied "I'm doing pretty well." And the individual asked me, "Well, why is that?" And I said, "Because I woke up today. I always think that's a great way to start the day off, don't ya think?" as I chuckled.

I didn't always operate with this mindset until I began looking at each new day as a new opportunity. New day, new opportunity. New day, new opportunity to be better than I was yesterday. New day, new opportunity to work toward a goal. New day, new opportunity to focus on loving myself. New day, new opportunity to build myself up. New day, new opportunity to get one step closer to all that I want out of life. So, no matter how many "Ls" you may take or how many times you may fail in life, be thankful that each new day comes with a new opportunity.

And when times get rough, I like to remind myself of this: Things that appear to be falling apart may just be falling into place!

*"Gratitude makes sense of our past, brings peace for today,*
*and creates a vision for tomorrow."*
—MELODY BEATTIE

THE WORLD IS A BETTER PLACE WITH YOU IN IT!

## CHAPTER AFFIRMATION

I am thankful for all the blessings which I see and don't see!

## WRITE YOUR OWN GRATITUDE

- I am grateful for_____

  _____!

- I am thankful for _____

  _____!

- I am glad to have _____

  _____ in my life!

- I am glad I woke up today because _____

  _____!

- I am proud of myself for_____

  _____!

# RESOURCES

*https://FindAHelpline.com/i/iasp*

For US and non-US residents, please visit *https://FindAHelp-line.com/i/iasp,* insert your country, and click "Search for Helplines" to be directed to available resources in your area. This website provides free, confidential support from a real human over phone, text, or webchat.

# CHAPTER 6

# UNIQUELY YOU

---

*"Be healthy and take care of yourself, but be happy with the beautiful things that make you, you."*
—BEYONCÉ

I remember I used to not love my body. I didn't even like my body.

I was super skinny, and I looked nothing like what I wanted to body-wise. I wanted muscles, bigger arms, a bigger chest to not only attract women but also to feel comfortable and confident when I took my shirt off. I had these feelings of insecurity for a while. The summer after my junior year of high school, I decided I was going to change things. I was tired of being so small and weak.

I decided I was going to actually start working out so I could get the body I wanted. All I had to work with were a couple of dumbbells my dad had and my body. Still, I knew this was something I needed to do to feel better about myself. So, I started training. Every day, I would wake up and get to working out. I did what seemed like countless curls, shoulder shrugs, and pushups, hoping to bulk up my scrawny frame.

Growing up, my dad used to do this thing where during every commercial break he would do push-ups, sit-ups, or flutter kicks, so I followed in his footsteps. Every time a commercial came on the TV, I would drop to the floor and do as many sit ups as I could before my show came back on. It didn't matter what time of day it was—whether it was 2:00 p.m. or 2:00 a.m. All that mattered to me was getting in shape.

It wasn't long after I started working out before my body began to break down on me, fatigued and exhausted.

I was doing all this work, all of these exercises every day that summer for weeks, and didn't see any progress. I became discouraged as I obsessively looked in the mirror each day and after each exercise.

*Why isn't anything happening?*

*Why aren't I getting bigger?*

*Where are the gains?*

*Why don't I see it going anywhere?*

*Am I doing this all in vain?*

I was really ready to give up. It felt like I had wasted all my time. I decided to give it a little more time. Maybe I was being impatient. I told myself if nothing changed in the next three weeks, I was done. So I continued to push myself to keep at it. The only thing driving me was just how bad I wanted it—to finally feel good about how I looked.

The first week went by and nothing changed. The second week went by, and I still felt the same. But a few days before the end of the third week, I started to notice something. I was no longer getting tired as easily or as quickly as I was before. As small as it might have seemed, I grasped onto this tiny bit of hope and held onto it for dear life. I was honestly really proud of myself.

Some form of validation or progress was all I needed to keep me going. Now that I had it, I wasn't going to stop.

I decided to stop spending so much time checking the mirror after every exercise and instead focus my attention on doing the work.

I started being able to do five more curls each set, ten more push-ups here, fifteen more sit-ups there. I no longer needed the instant gratification because of how good I felt hitting these small, attainable goals. What started out as a physical journey turned into a mental one. And the more work, time, and energy I invested in myself, the more I began to appreciate my body. The results of the journey gave me fulfillment.

After a while, working out became a habit for me and carried into the school year. Monday through Friday, I'd leave school and go straight to the gym. My routine of always checking the mirror was replaced with affirmations, especially on days where I would still find myself struggling with my body image. I'd take the time to remind myself to acknowledge my improvements, treat and celebrate myself, and list out qualities I liked about myself.

It wasn't until about a year later that I started to love myself wholeheartedly. I had to spend time with myself in order to become comfortable with who I was. At that point, I was content with where I was and was looking forward to where I was going. Now a high school senior, this once small, weak boy loved and appreciated the body he had worked so hard to get. And to make a good situation even better, that same young boy won the school's Most Athletic superlative that year.

As I was reflecting on my own story of where I was and where I am now, I came across Andrea Shaker, a fellow author in my book-writing program who happened to be a licensed professional counselor. I was really impressed with her background and felt like she could help add value to the content of my book. So, I reached out to her on LinkedIn and asked to interview her.

"I would love to!" Andrea cheerfully replied back.

As we were talking, I began to share some of my story while also listening to hers. Andrea told me that she used to struggle with self-love from a young age.

"I used to be really chubby as a younger kid, and I remember I always had body-image issues even back then. I was bullied. I absolutely hated trying on clothes. I didn't like society's view on telling me how I should look, and I didn't like that all women's clothes were tight fitted," Andrea recalls. For the longest time, she only wore baggy T-shirts and sweatpants because she didn't like what her body was.

In high school, Andrea had a growth spurt, began eating right and working out, and lost the weight. Yet, she would still have these thoughts. What she learned in adulthood is that it's not really about the body, it's more about your thoughts and your mindset toward yourself. It's more so about changing your thought process than your body.

"It took me a long time to realize this and feel this way, but your body is what makes you unique," Andrea said with a smile on her face. "You don't want to look like everybody else."

## YOU'RE WORTH IT! TIPS

### TIP #1: REMOVE SELF-DEPRECATION

Like affirmations, negative talk toward ourselves can alter our thoughts. However, unlike affirmations, self-deprecation negatively impacts our mental health. Be mindful of the words you use and how you speak about yourself. I was reading an interesting article from Well Being Trust that recommended you treat your body with the same kindness you'd treat a lifelong friend:

"If whatever you're about to say about your body is something you'd feel bad saying about a friend's body, then don't say it! You don't deserve verbal abuse from anybody, especially from yourself."

This article reminded me a lot of the call I was on with world-renowned brain coach and author of *New York Times* best seller *Limitless*, Jim Kwik. On our call, he said, "I believe your brain is like a supercomputer, and your self-talk is the program it will run. So if you tell yourself you're not good at remembering names, you won't remember the name of the next person you meet because you programmed your computer not to. People come to me all the time and say, 'Jim, I have horrible memory. Jim, I'm not smart enough. Jim, I'm too old.' I say stop. Control your self-talk because that's the program that'll run your mind. Your mind is always eavesdropping on your self-talk."

## TIP #2: PRACTICE SELF-CARE

There are a few ways you can practice self-care to promote your own positive body image. First, it's important to stop comparing yourself to others. We've all been guilty of scrolling on social media and comparing ourselves to others, wishing we looked like this person or that person. It quickly makes us question why we don't look a certain way and makes us feel bad about ourselves.

Clean your social media up and stop following people with unrealistic bodies or pages that make you feel bad. Instead, follow more body-positive pages or comedy pages. Social media used correctly should be a place for you to go to smile, laugh, and learn, not feel bad about yourself.

Other forms of self-care include complimenting your body every time you look in the mirror. Keep a list of things you like about yourself and your body. Every time a negative thought about your body pops into your mind, counter it with something positive. Fall in love with that person in the mirror.

### TIP #3: MOVE YOUR BODY

After you've made your list, move your body! You can exercise in the traditional sense at a gym, or you can hoop, swim, hike, dance, or play tennis. Regular exercise is good for the body and the mind, especially for those of us who stay up at night overthinking. According to sleep medicine psychologist Michelle Drerup, PsyD, at Cleveland Clinic, "When you exercise, your brain releases feel-good chemicals that combat stress and anxiety." This can lead to falling asleep faster and improved sleep quality. Not only will you ultimately look and feel better, but you'll also be able to watch yourself become a better version of you. Just don't forget to be patient with yourself and your progress.

Lastly, at the end of each week, take a day for you and do things that make you feel good about your body. This can be wearing your favorite clothes, doing photoshoots with friends, or—my personal favorite—listening to a soothing playlist as you unwind in a warm bubble bath.

### TIP #4: LOVE AND MEET YOURSELF WHERE YOU ARE

I'm here to let you know that you are more than enough as you are. Love yourself where you are now while working

SELF-CARE ISN'T SELFISH!

toward where you want to be physically, spiritually, mentally, and emotionally. Whether it's working toward your next physical goal or overcoming body image insecurities or loving yourself more, getting to your goal is a progression that doesn't happen overnight (but you will get there).

Just because you're not where you want to be doesn't mean the current version of you doesn't deserve love and attention. It's actually the opposite in that your current version needs to be showered with love and attention in order to blossom and grow into the version of you that you want to become. Also, don't fall into the trap of fake love from others. When we don't give ourselves the love and attention we deserve, it's easy to be drawn to individuals and situations that aren't good for us like a fly to a bright bug zapper.

Along with happiness and all the other things we've spoken on so far, self-love is something you work on every day. No matter where you are in your outward or inward appearance, be comfortable in your own skin and work on you. Your value is not measured in how others view you but in how YOU feel about yourself. You can love yourself as you continue to grow and develop in all aspects of your life.

We were taught by society to believe there's only one set standard or definition of beauty or attractiveness, and if we don't look like that one standard then we are not attractive or worthy of self-love. That couldn't be any further from the truth. Beauty actually comes in several different forms, and at the end of the day what makes you special and worthy of self-love is that you are uniquely you.

*"You are allowed to be both a masterpiece and a work in progress simultaneously."*
—SOPHIA BUSH

———

## CHAPTER AFFIRMATION

I love who I am and who I'm becoming unconditionally!

## WRITE YOUR OWN BODY-POSITIVE MESSAGES

- I like that I am _____

  _____!

- One of my best qualities is _____

  _____!

- I love myself because _____

  _____!

# CHAPTER 7

# PLANTING SEEDS

———

*"Nature herself does not distinguish between what seed it receives. It grows whatever seed is planted; this is the way life works. Be mindful of the seeds you plant today, as they will become the crop you harvest."*

—MARY MANIN MORRISSEY

Since freshman year of college, I had continued planting and feeding my poor habits. I didn't have any type of time-management skills, I didn't set or work toward any goals, and I procrastinated on everything. I even went as far as adopting the mantra of "due tomorrow, do tomorrow" where I would do an assignment on the day it was due.

My situation was a direct consequence of my actions, and these actions were leading me to a life of stress, hopelessness, and unhappiness. It was time to produce some new crops.

After three and a half years of constant stress from completing assignments last minute, I decided to switch things up and get more organized by putting myself on a schedule. The plan was to be a lot more efficient with my time, beginning with waking up earlier. I had previously woken up only ten to fifteen minutes before my class each day, giving myself just enough time to brush my teeth and head out the door.

The first week of trying to implement my new schedule went like this:

- Day 1: I slept through every alarm.
- Day 2: The snooze button and I became very close friends.
- Day 3: I turned my phone off after the first alarm so my bed and I could resume our warm, cuddling session in peace.
- Day 4: I woke up on time but didn't get out of bed.
- Day 5: I woke up on time but thought to myself, *It's Friday... I'll just try starting again next week.*

Sunday night came and I had to give myself a quick pep talk: "C'mon, man. Let's go, bruh. We have to get up tomorrow. If you want new results, you gotta take new actions. The only way to get to the future and life you want for yourself is to begin by creating and doing what you need to do now." For good measure, I even went to bed as early as I could.

The next day, I had only snoozed one alarm and managed to roll myself out of bed. Definitely progress, so I'll take it. I looked out my window and marveled at this bright light. *Hmm, so that's what a sunrise looks like*, I thought to myself.

Still groggy, I wiped my eyes and decided it was time for me to get my day started.

Over the course of that week and the weeks following, it became easier and easier to consistently get up on time. And I was getting so much done. For the first time in my college career, I was actually finishing and turning my assignments in early.

Each day started like this: wake up, go to the bathroom, meditate, read, and then grab breakfast where I'd be able to unlock my phone for the first time. Before the new change, I couldn't even remember when the last time was that I had had breakfast or read a book. My dad told me to read more, so I decided to try it. He said that by reading every day, I would always be learning and better than I was yesterday, and he was absolutely right.

After grabbing my food, I'd find a spot to sit down and eat. As I ate, I'd catch up on and respond to emails and look at current events going on around the world before watching videos on different topics I was interested in. Once done, I'd head back to the dorm where I had anywhere from an hour and a half to three hours until my first class began. The past me would still be under the covers somewhere snoring.

Not yet used to waking up earlier, I initially wanted to be somewhere asleep like my former self, but that would defeat the purpose of what I was doing. Instead, I chose to knock out as many of my assignments for the week as I could. After my first class, I'd eat lunch with a friend or two in the dorm, watch a funny video, and then head out to sit through my last class for the day.

My evenings were always reserved for homework, but I found that, with an earlier start to my day, this was almost never necessary. Instead, I spent time improving my life in other ways—working out, checking in on my family, scheduling fun trips to explore the city during the weekend, and working toward personal goals I had set. I finally had time to work on myself.

As I continued to practice these new daily habits, I knew I was on the right path when I found myself having so much more energy, having more peace, feeling a lot more productive, and actually being on top of things. Once I learned there were simple things I could do to improve my situation and my future, this whole life thing started to turn around for the better.

## *YOU'RE WORTH IT!* TIPS

My last semester of undergrad was arguably my most important and transformative semester. I started getting up earlier, meditating, reading a lot more, setting goals for myself, and working toward those goals every day. Prior to this, I never felt like I had any time; everything was always so rushed, which left me in a constant state of panic and anxiety. I was never doing any of the things I wanted to do. I wasn't working toward my goals. I was so flooded and overwhelmed by everything else that I didn't even know if I had any goals I wanted to work toward; my only goal was surviving the week, making it to the weekend, and then repeating the process all over again. Had I continued on the same path, I never would've graduated college or taken back control of my time.

The tips I'm about to share with you are the same methods I use today and the same methods that helped me graduate from Georgetown University in a semester where I was taking six classes and working a job. I want you to take back control of your life, plant the seeds for your growth, set goals, and create actionable steps that help you move toward your goals each day. May you find balance and peace in all aspects of your life and go from "busy and stressed" to "productive and blessed."

## TIP #1: BE PURPOSEFUL WITH YOUR TIME

From my earliest days on campus, I'd procrastinate. I'd wait until the last minute, become lazy, want more time, and then rush to throw something together. But what if there was a way to break the cycle? We all know about this dangerous cycle and yet we still procrastinate—even me in my "due tomorrow, do tomorrow" mentality from my first semester of college.

I sat down and spoke with Millicent Sykes, a practicing clinical counseling trainee (PCCT) and former brain stimulation technician, who said, "One habit that tends to encourage the procrastination or lack of fulfillment of one's goals is becoming overwhelmed by the emotions."

We'll feel stressed, have things to do, and know we have to do them but don't want to. It's in these moments where we may turn to unhelpful habits such as socializing or mindlessly scrolling through social media as a way to distract ourselves and keep us from thinking about our responsibilities.

The biggest thing that kept me from reverting back to bad habits was creating a schedule and system best fitted to me that walked me through my day from start to finish. Millicent took it a step further by pointing out the importance of instilling creativity and fun into whatever schedule you create.

In order to capitalize on and make the most out of your twenty-four hours, you want to create a schedule and start earlier on the things you have to do, but you also want to dedicate time to the things you are passionate about and enjoy. If you're like me, this can be making time to watch comedy stand-ups and anime in between assignments. If you're like Millicent, this can be writing a poem or working on a short story. It's harder to find excitement or drive when we are boggled down and so heavily entrenched in the details of deadlines and work, but it helps us find motivation and balance when we are more purposeful in making time to do the things we love.

At the end of the day, life is more than just work, work, work all the time. Life is meant to be enjoyed!

## TIP #2: SET SHORT AND LONG-TERM GOALS

Before you write down your goals, you have to believe they will come into fruition.

Toss out the idea of "impossible" because limits are nothing but fake restraints put on us by society, others who don't want to see you win, and sometimes ourselves—yes, even us when we self-sabotage and self-destruct our own goals and missions because we don't feel like we deserve to be happy. I'm here to let you know that you do deserve happiness and all that you want out of life.

An instrumental way to give yourself the future you want is by setting both short- and long-term goals. Start by setting a six-month, one-year, and five-year goal, and work your way backward (I'll explain what it means to work your way backward in the next tip). Create goals that inspire and motivate you to want to get up each day and go after them.

Our daily habits and consistency in them determine who we are and who we'll become more than anything. What you do today determines where you'll be tomorrow. You want to make sure your daily actions and habits relate to your goals, and remove the ones that don't. Write down the top three things you want to accomplish tomorrow before you go to bed. In doing this, your subconscious will know where your focus for tomorrow lies, and it'll help you get so much more done. Think of these as mini goals that will snowball into one of your larger goals. If you want to lose five pounds, one of these three accomplishments may be working out tomorrow.

You may not be able to do everything all at once, but in tackling your mini goals, you'll start to feel accomplished and see new movement in your life. I want to remind you that it's okay to have a bad day here and there while you're trying to achieve new goals. Just get back up and keep going.

## TIP #3: 'BOUT THAT ACTION

A question I often ask myself is, *What are you doing today to get to where you want to be tomorrow?* I had finally made goals to go after but didn't know where or how to start. I was what I call a "lister." I'd write down a list of everything to do but then I'd get stuck in this preparatory stage and never actually start anything. Then after that list was done, I'd go and make a whole other list and once again not execute anything. *What's wrong with me?* I would think. *Why can't I ever start or finish anything?*

If you've ever faced a similar situation, there's actually nothing wrong with us but rather how we approach taking action. I discovered that the biggest factors keeping me from starting were feeling overwhelmed by the task at hand and always wanting everything to be perfect. So how do we get over this? I'll tell you.

First, start where you are! Perfectionism produces inactivity. Everything doesn't have to be perfect for you to begin.

Of course, preparation is important, but if you're waiting to start that business you've been wanting to start because of something as trivial as not having the right name or slogan, then that's counterproductive. The best way to not be inactive is to get started where you are.

Now, to get started on what seems to be a daunting task or goal, you should break it down into actionable steps. Every mile can be broken down into inches, and every year can be broken down into seconds. No matter how big the obstacle ahead may seem, you can break it down into something more approachable. Be "'bout that action" and split your tasks, projects, and assignments up in a way that gives you a better chance to take action. For example, a goal of mine was to write a book. Just saying it out loud can be scary and sound overwhelming. Honestly having goals that scare us should actually excite us. So I decided to write a book. No one in my family has written a book, and I had never written a book; I can barely write a decent paper on a good day.

Now that I have my end goal of writing a book in mind, what *actionable* steps can I take to get to it? First, I could reach out to someone who's written a book before and has a book-writing program. My second actionable step could then be thinking of a topic to speak on and write about. My next step could then be deciding what story I'd like to share first. I don't just tackle the whole book head on at once but break it down into actionable steps that get me started. I take it one chapter at a time and make progress toward what I want to achieve until I have a book. Had I gotten hung up on everything being perfect, I would've spent months just twiddling my thumbs trying to decide on the perfect title and not getting anything done.

By breaking your goals into smaller, actionable steps, your subconscious mind is now better able to focus without feeling so overwhelmed. Not only that, but it's a great feeling crossing something off your to do list, no matter how small; it makes you feel accomplished and one step closer to your goal, because you are!

*"Goal setting is a powerful tool and process for motivating you. When effective goals are set, a giant step toward the life you desire is taken."*

—K.C. ROWNTREE

---

## CHAPTER AFFIRMATION

I am in control of my time and my life!

## WRITE YOUR OWN ACTION PLAN

One of my personal goals as mentioned before was writing a book. What is a goal you want to achieve? Now, let's work backward from that goal to create a roadmap in order to achieve it. What actionable steps will lead you to your goal? Remember, it's all about looking at where you want to be, working backward, and planting the seeds of your success now. After you've written down your actionable steps, execute and create a life for yourself that future you will look back on and thank you for!

Actionable Step #1: _____

_____

Actionable Step #2: _____

_____

Actionable Step #3: _____

_____

Actionable Step #4: _____

_____

Actionable Step #5: _____

_____

Actionable Step #6: _____

_____

Actionable Step #8: _____

_____

Actionable Step #9: _____

_____

Actionable Step #10: _____

_____

GOAL: _____

_____

# RESOURCES

*https://YouTube.com/c/Psych2go*

One of my favorite YouTube channels I like to watch is called Psych2Go. They provide a lot of entertaining content around mental health that is extremely helpful. You should definitely check them out!

# CHAPTER 8

# GROW AT YOUR OWN PACE

———

*"A flower does not think of competing
with the flower next to it. It just blooms."*
—ZEN SHIN

Ever since I was little, I've never been "Mr. Popular" or really ever belonged to any group or clique.

I've always been nerdy and mocked on several occasions for "being different." I wanted all the friends and popularity the cool kids had. I wanted their life and to be them. This way of thinking continued into high school and college and only worsened the more I looked and compared my life and situation to what I saw on social media.

All of a sudden, my life wasn't looking so good anymore, and envy turned to sadness each time I hopped on my phone. *But*

*I could still have lots of friends, right? Maybe that would make me feel better*, I convinced myself.

On campus, I'd go talk to anyone and always try to be friends with everyone, seeking to one day be cool and popular and have all those friends like I saw when I was little. And for some time, it seemed to be working. I felt like I was getting the validation I wanted. I knew a lot of people and a lot of people knew me, so they must've liked me, right? I felt like I was fitting in and on my way to being one of the cool kids.

But one day, I was walking on one side of the street and waved to someone I knew, and they acted as if they didn't see me. I wasn't sure what that was about, but it sparked a revelation in me. This wasn't the first time this had happened, and I noticed I was always the one to initiate conversations and interactions, not just with this person but with most people I knew. I was always the first one to wave and say hello in order to get a response back. I decided to put it to the test, and almost immediately as I stopped waving and initiating everything, I began to see how many empty relationships I had been supporting.

I was confused. What did I do for them to not like me?

For the longest time, I had felt like having a lot of friends who approved of me would make me happy. I had spent so much time and energy trying to impress people who didn't care anything about me or even like me. And to make matters worse, I still wanted to be like the same people who shunned me and have the lives of those I saw on social media.

I'd see this person getting this internship, that person getting this job offer, and this person over here getting to travel to this country. It seems like things were going great for everyone except for me. Yes it's good to see others do well, but when was it going to be my turn? The more validation I sought and the more I compared myself to others, the more inadequate I felt and as though my own accomplishments weren't enough. I felt as if I wasn't enough.

After noticing the imbalanced dynamics of these poor relationships, I stopped waving. I stopped trying so hard to fit into situations where I wasn't wanted or felt like I had to force my way in.

It wasn't too long after that when I found my tribe, my two closest friends on campus—Derrick and Steven.

The first time I met Derrick was the last night of NSO. We introduced ourselves and sparked up a quick conversation while we ate tacos by the taco truck before calling it a night. Steven and I had met and interacted a few times in a program we were both members of.

What was different about these two was just how genuine and real each of them were—something that seemed rare to find those days. After introducing them to one another, the three of us would get lunch and dinner together every day. We'd crack jokes, talk about our shared interests, and tell stories. And our friendship naturally grew into a brotherhood the more we hung out.

I didn't have to have all the friends in the world, and I didn't need to either because I had true friends who appreciated and valued me for me. Being in an environment like that where I could be who I was and they could be who they were made me a lot more secure in myself. And being myself allowed me to see the best parts of me and know that I was enough.

## YOU'RE WORTH IT! TIPS

### TIP #1: QUALITY OVER QUANTITY

Like all investments in life, quality is better than quantity. This is also true of your circle and those you decide to surround yourself with. When I was in school, I wanted to have all the friends in the world, thinking that the quantity would make me happier. What I actually uncovered was that I never really had a lot of friends but a lot of associates. Now, you may be asking yourself, *Well, what's the difference?*

An associate is someone who doesn't have your best interests in mind. They talk about you behind your back, they're negative toward you, and they're energy vampires. Energy vampires are people who cast doubt and negative energy your way and on your dreams because they're afraid of the potential you have inside (that you might not even see yet). You always seem to feel drained of energy after speaking with them or after each interaction. Those who fake smile in your face don't belong in your life.

You want to surround yourself with quality, genuine people who truly care about you and your wellbeing. They are solid individuals who motivate you and celebrate your wins and successes as if they were their own. Real friends are there for you when you need them, encourage you, check up on you, help you grow, and bring positive energy. It's a mutually beneficial relationship. When it comes to choosing your friends, choose quality and those who add value and happiness to your life.

## TIP #2: TAKE A SOCIAL MEDIA BREAK

More now than ever with the internet and social media, it's so easy to compare ourselves. The fact that we have technology that can bring society's idea of perfection to us in the manner that it's being brought to us right now is huge. The impact of being able to compare ourselves on the scale and the level we're doing it at is unreal.

After I saw the negative effect social media was having on my mental health, I decided to take a year off. I felt so much more peace and sure of myself once I did, and it allowed me to step back, self-reflect, and practice more gratitude in my own life as I got to know myself.

When I was about to make my return to social media, I began thinking of ways I could more intentionally use it as a helpful and positive tool rather than a detrimental one. The first thing I did and recommend is removing pages that make you feel down and don't add any value or happiness to your life. Follow pages that make you laugh and smile, pages that help you learn, and pages that encourage and uplift you to become your best self.

## TIP #3: THE PERSPECTIVE THAT CHANGED
## MY ENTIRE WAY OF THINKING

One simple perspective that changed my entire way of thinking was brought upon by this question: What does someone else's opinion of you have to do with your success?

And the answer is absolutely nothing. No one else's opinion of you has any effect on the success of your life. I'm going to say that again. No one else's opinion of you has any effect on the success of *your* life!

As soon as I comprehended this concept, my mindset shifted, and I became so much happier as a result. It no longer mattered what negative things people had to say about me or what they thought of me for "always being different" because their words had no impact on who I was and the life I was working to achieve for myself. I control the outcome of my life and my situation, and everything I want out of life is attainable. You control the outcome of your life and your situation, and everything you want out of life is attainable.

Now watch this. People who judge you are so focused on your life that they're not getting any closer to their goals. But the same is true for the opposite. When I was focused so much on what others were doing and what others thought of me, I wasn't getting any closer to living the life I wanted for myself. The energy you are putting into other people and things that don't matter shouldn't be going into you, your growth, and your development. There's always going to be someone hating on you. Cool. Let them hate. Let people do them, and you do you.

You don't have to impress anyone else. The only validation you need is from yourself. So the next time you feel like someone doesn't like you or is talking badly about you, ask yourself, Does this person's opinion of me have anything to do with my success and the goals I'm working to achieve? And after you answer no, focus on finding happiness in your true authentic self and work even harder to get to where you want to be in all aspects of your life.

## TIP #4: YOU HAVE TIME

It's okay to not have everything figured out right now. Most don't. Just focus on progress because no one has ever achieved greatness with complacency. So for each time you may stumble backward, take two steps forward. One step back, two steps forward. That's movement; that's progress. There's a lot more good in front of you that far outweighs the bad behind you.

Whether you're in the left lane or the far right lane, we're all going to get to our destinations. You are not behind in life, and you don't have to put so much pressure on yourself to figure everything out right now, because time is on your side. As long as you are making progress, then you are moving at the right speed. You are stepping into who you are to become. So be patient with yourself as you grow at your own pace.

BE PATIENT WITH YOURSELF!

*"Be patient with yourself. You are growing stronger every day. The weight of the world will become lighter... and you will begin to shine brighter. Don't give up."*

—ROBERT TEW

## CHAPTER AFFIRMATION

I am growing at my own pace!

## WRITE YOUR OWN FOCUS

- I will not worry about other people's lives because I am

  focused on _____

  _____!

- Others' opinions of me will not keep me from achieving

  _____

  _____!

- As I grow at my own pace, I know I will successfully ___

  _____

  _____!

# CONCLUSION

---

Halfway through writing this book, my mom asked me a question that she hadn't really asked in a while: "Tre', are you happy?"

Once again, it caught me off guard. I looked her in eyes and resoundingly replied, "Yes, I am."

There was no over-the-top fanfare, but her smile said it all as we continued our conversation.

I was someone who had hit their lowest point in life a few years ago. It was in that moment that I made a promise to myself I would never go back to that dark place again. Most of the time, a lot of our growth comes from when our backs are against the wall because it pushes us to new levels.

I started shifting my mindset and implementing new changes in my life which you now know as the affirmations and *You're Worth It!* Tips.

I know what it's like to feel as if absolutely nothing is going your way—to feel anxious, insecure, and behind in life. Yes, life can seem overwhelming at times. But even with all this, my imperfect self has overcome and found my value and worth, and you can too.

You should be proud of yourself for finishing this entire book. You have just taken the first step to prioritizing yourself, your peace, your mental health, your happiness, and your growth. Now it's time to apply everything you've learned to your daily life.

You are in control of your life. Use the affirmations. Use the tips. Use the resources. They're all there for your benefit.

Know that your mind is the greatest asset you have, and it's important for you to protect and nurture it.

Take the time to learn, understand, and embrace yourself. Play more of an active role in your life by purposefully doing more of what you truly enjoy and what makes you happy. Chill, enjoy life, and find things and people who make you laugh and smile. Whatever it is that puts a smile on your face and brings you fulfillment, make sure you're incorporating more of that into your daily and weekly schedule.

Lastly, work on yourself every single day. Work on loving yourself. Work on expressing gratitude. Work on overcoming your fears. Like any other goal, everything that you want out of life is on the other side of consistency and discipline.

The journey isn't always easy, so please be patient with yourself as you grow and develop in all aspects of your life because *You're Worth It!*

---

## CHAPTER AFFIRMATION

I'm worth it!

## RESOURCES

*YoureWorthItBook.com*

YoureWorthItBook.com is the official website for *You're Worth It!* Here, you'll be able to find additional resources, schedule speaking engagements with Tre' Bohannon, and keep up with the latest initiatives and events from *You're Worth It!*

# ACKNOWLEDGMENTS

---

I want to make sure I show my love and appreciation to everyone who supported me early on in this life-changing journey!

THANK YOU SO MUCH!!!

Adrian Abrams
Andrew Allen
Shanetrice Allen
Nate Alleyne
Alma Angel
Derrick Arthur-Cudjoe
Roberto and Lisa Ayala
Lacasa Bailey
Veronica Banks
Miles Barksdale
Derrick and Chelsea Bates
Sarah Bax
Eurika Beard
Darcy Bedford
Phyllis Bennett
James Berti

A'rmond Birmingham
Cirr-Nicholas Bohannon
Herbert Bohannon, Jr.
Justin Bohannon
Regenia Bohannon
Kimberly Boone
Genean Borne
Jeff and Kukie Boutte'
Dana Brown
Denzell Brown
Doris and Herschel Brown, MD
Jason and Traci Brown
Joshua Burke
Paulette Busby
Mannone Butler

Britney Lee Carter
Shomik Chakraborty
Kimberly Chanchavac
Shauntal Collins
Carl Corliss
Donal Cotter
James and Adela Cox
Ellen Crosier
Marquis Danner
Brian Davis
Christina Davis
Melba Davis
Noelle Dayal
Jared Daye
Valerie Daye
AJ Dudley
Vanessa Ellis
Isaac Ellsworth
Faith Temple Conquerors
Pathfinder Club
Aubrey Favors
Christy Felix
Noah Fenstermacher
German Figuero
Dr. Rolanda Findlay
Glorian Ford
Zenobia Fortune
Jay Foster
Sharif Fotouh
Missy Foy
Eaujenae Francisco
Joe Garfola

Daivon Gatling-Tillery
Saba Ghebreyesus
Jason Gold
Ronnie and Connie Green
Antonio Griffith
Jo Guthrie
Sky Harrison
Chase Hawthorne
Sarajane Hodges
Saniyah Hoodye
Tammy Hubbard
Monique Hucks
Carol Huffman
Wesley Hughes
Woodley Jean-Louis
Kieran Jenkins
Reezan Jiwa
Darlene Johnson
Dennis Johnson
Frederick Johnson
Vernon and Vickie Johnson
Vernon Johnson II
Bob Jones
Rickey Jordan
Princesse Karemera
David Kelley
Lexi Kimball
Eric Koester
Conya Kossie
Sienzhi Kouemo
David Larsen
Mikey Lepard

Nigel Lewis
Toni Ligons
Miguel and Naya Lopez
Kamar Mack
Danielle Maduka
Johnathan Mark
Debra Mason
Keshia Mason
Caleb Mathis
Courtney Mathis
Robert and Lawana Mathis
Robert Mathis, Jr.
Regan McCune
Maria McPhaull
Kenneth Medlock
Johnny and Yolanda Mickens
Teresa Mitchell-Monroe
Kevin Mondy, Sr.
Ronnie Moore
Stevie and Monica Moore
Darrell Morgan
Barbara Morris
Steven Mucyo
Jackie Nash
Nate Neugebauer
Sherri Nichelson
Sam O'Connell
Darius Okafor
Gregg and Kim Oliphant
Gerardo Padierna
Daniel Park
Marco Paternoster

Kevin Perry
Evan Pham
Meleena Phillips
Rashad Pitts
Aaron Powell
Clarence Powell
Camryn Privette
Project Still I Rise
Luisa Ramondo
Kerry and Tana Ranking
Samson Rao
Spencer Ray
Renzo Reyes
Lamont Reynolds
Kyrsten Rice
James and Denise Roberts
Terrence Roberts
Marcus Robinson
Chase Rollins
Carlos Rosario
Leonard Ross
Rob Roudebush
Jim and Cynthia Scales
Melody Scott
Andrea Shaker
Emory Siedell
Trenyse Small
Dorian Smith
Myiah Smith
Terrence Southern
Kimberly Stewart
Tanya Stewart

Trent Stewart
Millicent Sykes
Jennie Tai
Broc Taylor
Maxine Theriot
Carroll Thomas
Cynthia Thomas
Kesha Thomas
Carlos Tilliman
Jade Tucker
Andrea Vox-Afful
Amanda Wade

Dr. Jo Ellyn Walker
Glen Waters
Brooks Watson
Sharon Watson
Maxim Wheatley
Tenacia Whiteside
Shonda Wilbon
Gloria Williams
Toni Williams
Derek and Sylvia Woodson
Shirjuanda Woodson

# APPENDIX

---

## INTRODUCTION:

Magellan Health Insights. "7 Mental health myths and facts." Accessed November 11, 2020. *https://magellanhealthinsights. com/2018/05/23/7-mental-health-myths-and-facts.*

## CHAPTER 1:

CNBC Make It. "51% of young Americans say they feel down, depressed or hopeless—here's how advocates are trying to help." Accessed November 11, 2020. *https://www.cnbc. com/2021/05/10/51percent-of-young-americans-say-they-feel-down-depressed-or-hopeless.html.*

Healthline. "Anxiety Exercises to Help You Relax." Accessed November 11, 2020. *https://www.healthline.com/health/anxiety-exercises.*

Healthline. "How to Craft and Use Affirmations for Anxiety." Accessed November 11, 2020. *https://www.healthline.com/ health/mental-health/affirmations-for-anxiety.*

Verywell Mind. "8 Deep Breathing Exercises to Reduce Anxiety." Accessed November 11, 2020. *https://www.verywellmind.com/ abdominal-breathing-2584115.*

**CHAPTER 2:**

TED. "How to fix a broken heart | Guy Winch." February 27, 2018. Video, 12:25. *https://youtu.be/koGQSJrpVhM.*

**CHAPTER 3:**

HelpGuide. "Helping Someone Who's Grieving." Accessed November 11, 2020. *https://www.helpguide.org/articles/grief/helping-someone-who-is-grieving.htm.*

**CHAPTER 4:**

Verywell Mind. "What Is Meditation?" Accessed November 11, 2020. *https://www.verywellmind.com/what-is-meditation-2795927.*

**CHAPTER 6:**

Cleveland Clinic. "How Exercise Affects Your Sleep." Accessed November 11, 2020. *https://health.clevelandclinic.org/how-exercise-affects-your-sleep.*

Well Being Trust. "10 Ways to Practice Body Positivity." Accessed November 11, 2020. *https://wellbeingtrust.org/news/10-ways-to-practice-body-positivity.*